WINNER TAKES ALL

Quizbook

Based on the television programme
devised by Geoffrey Wheeler
and presented by Jimmy Tarbuck

Questions by Deborah Sutherland

Ward Lock Limited · London

© Quiz Format Geoffrey Wheeler 1980
© Questions Deborah Sutherland 1980
© Winner Takes All, Trident Television Ltd 1980

First published in Great Britain in 1980
by Ward Lock Limited, 116 Baker Street,
London W1M 2BB, a Pentos Company.

Printed and bound in Great Britain by
C. Nicholls & Company, The Philips Park Press, Manchester.

British Library Cataloguing in Publication Data

Winner takes all quizbook.
  1. Questions and answers
  793.7'3   AG195

ISBN 0-7063-6072-9

How to play 'Winner Takes All'

This is a game for any number of players. One person who is not playing should act as quizmaster so that fair play is ensured when looking up the answers at the back of the book.

System 1 This is very similar to the method used in the television programme. Each player begins the game with 100 points. When a question is asked each person chooses one of the six possible answers and 'bets' a number of points. If the correct answer has been picked that player wins the points risked multiplied by the number of points the answer carries and, of course, gets back the points betted. If the answer is wrong the player loses only the number of points he or she has betted. Thus if one person bets 10 points on an answer which carries a score of 3, he or she will win 30 points if the answer is correct, or lose 10 points if it is wrong.

System 2 This is a simpler method. Again each player begins the game with 100 points. As each question is asked every player picks an answer and wins or loses the score which that answer carries, depending on whether the answer is right or wrong.

Each individual game contains 3 questions. The players may continue from game to game through the whole book or consider 3 games to equal one whole match which can be won or lost.

Any player who loses all his or her points is out of the game.

The winner is the player who has won most points at the end of play.

How to make a 'Winner Takes All' scorecard

All that is required is a small notebook with spiral-binding along the top, a pair of scissors and a felt-tipped pen. Using 10 pages of the notebook, divide each into 3 strips cutting from the bottom of each page up to the binding. Do not remove the pages from the notebook. On the first page write three noughts in a row, one on each strip. On the second page write three 1s and on the third page three 2s. Do this until you reach the tenth page which will carry three 9s. Turn the strips to show 100. By turning over the strips as you win or lose points, you will be able to keep your own score. For example, if one player begins by winning 10 points he or she will turn over the middle strip to a 1 and the score will read 110.

Who invented the fictional
character of Tarzan?

0 Charles Darwin
2 E. R. Burroughs
3 Desmond Morris
4 Rider Haggard
5 John Buchan
10 Elaine Morgan

What would you do
with a brad?

0 Eat it
2 Polish it
3 Write on it
4 Cook with it
5 Hit it
10 Burn it

Who was the mother
of Oedipus?

0 Helen
2 Jocasta
3 Leda
4 Ismene
5 Antigone
10 Eurydice

How far is a
kilometre?

0 .62 mile

2 ½ mile

3 3 miles

4 5½ miles

5 1 mile

10 .26 mile

Where is the
Humboldt Current?

0 Pacific Ocean

2 Aegean Sea

3 Arctic Ocean

4 Bering Sea

5 Caribbean Sea

10 Atlantic Ocean

How much was a
groat?

0 Twopence (2d/1p)

2 Sixpence (6d/2½p)

3 Fourpence (4d/1½p)

4 Farthing (¼d)

5 Threepence (3d/1p)

10 Two shillings (2s/10p)

Which of these men
was born in Georgia?

0 Franklin Roosevelt
2 Winston Churchill
3 Joseph Stalin
4 Thomas Jefferson
5 Theodore Roosevelt
10 Abraham Lincoln

What is the chief interest
of a speleologist?

0 Mirrors
2 Caves
3 Jewellery
4 Spells
5 Conversations
10 Silverwork

What is the food colouring
cochineal made from?

0 Tree
2 Beetle
3 Fruit
4 Leaf
5 Root
10 Flower

Bathsheba's first husband was Uriah the Hittite.
Who was her second husband?

0 Zadok
2 King David
3 Absalom
4 King Solomon
5 Nathan
10 Jehoshaphat

What was the stage name of
Frances Gumm?

0 Joan Crawford
2 Marilyn Monroe
3 Gloria Grahame
4 Judy Garland
5 Rhonda Fleming
10 Ginger Rogers

Who is most likely to use
a Wardian case?

0 Solicitor
2 Anatomist
3 Ceramicist
4 Fern collector
5 Bus conductor
10 Roof tiler

To which island was Napoleon sent
in August 1815?
- **0** St Helena
- **2** Ascension Island
- **3** Elba
- **4** Easter Island
- **5** St Kitts
- **10** Seychelles

Which of these countries has both an Atlantic
and Pacific seaboard?
- **0** Surinam
- **2** Venezuela
- **3** Ecuador
- **4** Guyana
- **5** Colombia
- **10** Peru

Which of Shaw's plays opens with the words,
'No eggs! No eggs!'?
- **0** *Saint Joan*
- **2** *Pygmalion*
- **3** *Heartbreak House*
- **4** *Man and Superman*
- **5** *Candida*
- **10** *The Applecart*

Which spice is a vital ingredient of Hungarian goulash?

0 Nutmeg
2 Cinnamon
3 Ginger
4 Paprika
5 Mace
10 Turmeric

Who was British Prime Minister in 1936?

0 Stanley Baldwin
2 Lloyd George
3 Clement Attlee
4 Ramsay MacDonald
5 Neville Chamberlain
10 Emmanuel Shinwell

What is the smallest resident British bird?

0 Linnet
2 Goldcrest
3 Blue tit
4 Jenny wren
5 Dunnock
10 Chaffinch

Which acid is present in the majority
of car batteries?

0 Phosphoric acid
2 Sulphuric acid
3 Oxalic acid
4 Nitric acid
5 Hydrochloric acid
10 Acetic acid

Who, in 973, was crowned first King
of the English in Bath?

0 Harold
2 Edgar
3 Alfred
4 Aethelstan
5 Edmund
10 Aethelred

Which part of the human body contains two bones
called the hammer and anvil?

0 Ear
2 Fourth finger
3 Eye
4 Thumb
5 Foot
10 Knee

Which saint's day falls on
11 November?
0 St Stephen
2 St Martin
3 St Giles
4 St Luke
5 St Bartholomew
10 St Nicholas

On which part of the body were pattens
once worn?
0 Ears
2 Feet
3 Hands
4 Thighs
5 Shins
10 Shoulders

Which country had a new monarch in
January 1972?
0 Denmark
2 Belgium
3 Norway
4 Spain
5 Sweden
10 Greece

In which year was
the battle of Marston Moor?

0 1698
2 1604
3 1684
4 1644
5 1623
10 1632

Who is the suitor of Katherina in Shakespeare's
The Taming of the Shrew?

0 Valentine
2 Claudio
3 Petruchio
4 Proteus
5 Angelo
10 Antonio

What is tritium?

0 Metal
2 Chemical compound
3 Metallic alloy
4 Isotope of hydrogen
5 Heavy gas
10 Liquid substance

What is the former name of
the River Severn?

0 Seven
2 Sefen
3 Midwin
4 Seph
5 Sabrina
10 Ouse

What is a trichologist
particularly interested in?

0 Hens
2 Hair
3 Magic
4 Knitting
5 Book-binding
10 Tricycles

Of which country is
Mogadishu the capital?

0 Chile
2 Khmer Republic
3 Albania
4 Dahomey
5 Bhutan
10 Somalia

Who was the founder
of Detroit?
- **0** Antoine Cadillac
- **2** Henry Knox
- **3** Chief Pontiac
- **4** Aaron Burr
- **5** James Madison
- **10** John Marshall

What was a clepsydra
used for?
- **0** Laying and fixing carpets
- **2** Turning a mill wheel
- **3** Brushing curly hair
- **4** Telling the time by water
- **5** Fixing buttons on an overall
- **10** Removing warts

What is the approximate weight of
the shuttle in badminton?
- **0** 16 gm
- **2** 5 gm
- **3** 2 gm
- **4** $\frac{1}{2}$ gm
- **5** 26 gm
- **10** 1 gm

When, approximately,
was the Jockey Club founded?
 0 1910
 2 1750
 3 1830
 4 1630
 5 1866
10 1894

In which constellation is the
bright star Rigel?
 0 Cassiopeia
 2 Cygnus
 3 Orion
 4 Aquila
 5 Sagittarius
10 Canis Major

In which country do most of the
inhabitants speak Amharic?
 0 Liberia
 2 Bahrain
 3 Togo
 4 Ethiopia
 5 Oman
10 Bhutan

What herb, sometimes used in cookery,
has the Latin name *Artemesia dracunculus*?

- **0** Thyme
- **2** Dill
- **3** Tarragon
- **4** Rosemary
- **5** Marjoram
- **10** Fennel

If you consulted *Bradshaw's Guide*,
what would you be interested in?

- **0** Railway timetables
- **2** Sports records
- **3** Biographies
- **4** Recipes
- **5** Shells
- **10** Rose trees

Who was the first woman Member of Parliament
to sit in the House of Commons?

- **0** Emmeline Pankhurst
- **2** Nancy Astor
- **3** Sophia Jex-Blake
- **4** Eleanor Rathbone
- **5** Elizabeth Garrett Anderson
- **10** Bessie Braddock

How many carats are there in
pure gold?

0 22
2 18
3 36
4 24
5 20
10 40

Which metal is known scientifically
by the symbol Hg?

0 Mercury
2 Lead
3 Antimony
4 Gold
5 Tin
10 Silver

What was a 'British Warm'?

0 An officer's thick overcoat
2 A fur muff
3 A pocket hot-water bottle
4 A kitchen range
5 A sailor's rum ration
10 A feather mattress

What is the raw material from which
sake is made?
- **0** Rice
- **2** Wheat
- **3** Seaweed
- **4** Barley
- **5** Potatoes
- **10** Grapes

What kind of pastry is used for
making eclairs?
- **0** Choux
- **2** Puff
- **3** Rich short
- **4** Flaky
- **5** Short
- **10** Rough puff

Who first calculated the circumference
of the Earth?
- **0** Tycho Brahe
- **2** Isaac Newton
- **3** Copernicus
- **4** Eratosthenes of Alexandria
- **5** Abdullah al Mamun
- **10** Leonardo da Vinci

In the Church of England,
who is the Primate of England?
- **0** Bishop of Winchester
- **2** Bishop of Bath and Wells
- **3** Archbishop of Canterbury
- **4** Archbishop of York
- **5** Bishop of Durham
- **10** Bishop of London

Which of these men served three terms as
President of the United States?
- **0** Lyndon Johnson
- **2** Calvin Coolidge
- **3** Theodore Roosevelt
- **4** Franklin Roosevelt
- **5** Thomas Jefferson
- **10** Harry Truman

Who wrote the poem which begins,
'Come live with me and be my love'?
- **0** Ben Jonson
- **2** Robert Herrick
- **3** Mick Jagger
- **4** William Shakespeare
- **5** Christopher Marlowe
- **10** Edmund Spenser

Which book has the subtitle
'The Modern Prometheus'?

 0 *Origin of Species*
 2 *A Canticle for Leibowitz*
 3 *The Female Eunuch*
 4 *The Day of the Triffids*
 5 *Nineteen Eighty-Four*
10 *Frankenstein*

(This is a soccer question)
Which country won the 1958 World Cup?

 0 Sweden
 2 Brazil
 3 Portugal
 4 West Germany
 5 Uruguay
10 England

Who wrote the poem entitled
'The Dreadful Story about Harriet
and the Matches'?

 0 Hilaire Belloc
 2 Lewis Carroll
 3 Harriet Beecher Stowe
 4 Edward Lear
 5 Heinrich Hoffman
10 Frances Hodgson Burnett

What is the popular name for
the garden shrub *Ribes sanguineum*?

0 Lilac
2 Flowering currant
3 Laburnum
4 Broom
5 Forsythia
10 Flowering cherry

In ancient Rome, which of these officials
was in charge of the Treasury?

0 Praetor
2 Consul
3 Censor
4 Aedile
5 Quaestor
10 Pro-Consul

What does the annual November parade
in Moscow celebrate?

0 The Great October Revolution of 1917
2 Birth of Lenin
3 Armistice Day 1918
4 The February Revolution of 1917
5 Death of the Tsar
10 The First Revolution of 1905

A deficiency of which of these vitamins
leads to the blood failing to clot in bleeding?
 0 Vitamin D
 2 Vitamin K
 3 Vitamin E
 4 Vitamin A
 5 Vitamin C
10 Vitamin B

Who built the Iron Bridge
across the River Severn in 1779?
 0 Robert Stephenson
 2 Isambard Kingdom Brunel
 3 Abraham Darby
 4 Thomas Telford
 5 Marc Isambard Brunel
10 John Rennie

What is the most northerly point
of the mainland of Britain?
 0 Strathy Point
 2 Dunnet Head
 3 John O'Groats
 4 Cape Wrath
 5 Whiten Head
10 Duncansby Head

Who died as a result of wearing
the shirt of Nessus?

0 Heracles
2 Aeneas
3 Theseus
4 Ajax
5 Atlas
10 Odysseus

When making fudge at home,
what temperature should the mixture be at
when you remove it from the heat?

0 220° F
2 350° F
3 310° F
4 290°F
5 238° F
10 254° F

Which planet was discovered in 1781?

0 Neptune
2 Uranus
3 Mars
4 Saturn
5 Pluto
10 Venus

Who wrote the poem which begins
'What passing-bells for these who die as cattle'?

- **0** Robert Graves
- **2** Wilfred Owen
- **3** W. B. Yeats
- **4** Rupert Brooke
- **5** W. H. Davies
- **10** Robert Bridges

What is a shaddock?

- **0** Leather apron
- **2** Heavy hammer
- **3** Tube in a television set
- **4** Citrus fruit
- **5** Hermit's hideout
- **10** Curtain in a church

Who was assassinated
by a man called Godse?

- **0** Leon Trotsky
- **2** Lord Moyne
- **3** Archduke Franz Ferdinand
- **4** Robert Kennedy
- **5** Gandhi
- **10** Abraham Lincoln

Which order built
Jervaulx Abbey?
0 Franciscans
2 Cistercians
3 Carmelites
4 Benedictines
5 Ursulines
10 Dominicans

Who starred in the film
Go West, Young Man?
0 Clara Bow
2 Jean Harlow
3 Gloria Swanson
4 Mae West
5 Pola Negri
10 Theda Bara

In motor racing who was
the Drivers World Champion in 1957?
0 Stirling Moss
2 Jack Brabham
3 Juan Manuel Fangio
4 Mike Hawthorn
5 Graham Hill
10 Phil Hill

Where was the earliest-known system of
shorthand invented and used?

- **0** Germany
- **2** Rome
- **3** USA
- **4** Scotland
- **5** France
- **10** Switzerland

Who starred in the film
High and Dizzy?

- **0** John Barrymore
- **2** Buster Keaton
- **3** Al Jolson
- **4** Harold Lloyd
- **5** Charlie Chaplin
- **10** Joe E. Brown

Which of these Irishmen
has won the Nobel Prize for Literature?

- **0** George Russell
- **2** J. M. Synge
- **3** Samuel Beckett
- **4** James Joyce
- **5** Oscar Wilde
- **10** Sean O'Casey

Which American industrial city stands at the confluence of the Allagheny and Monogahela rivers?

0 Columbus
2 Pittsburgh
3 Charleston
4 Cincinnati
5 Louisville
10 Philadelphia

What is a Lammergeier?

0 Saxon musical instrument
2 Tibetan cloak
3 Mythical beast
4 River insect
5 Policeman's truncheon
10 Bearded vulture

What, most commonly, is the meat basic to the dish called stroganoff?

0 Beef
2 Lamb
3 Pork
4 Duck
5 Veal
10 Mutton

What fruit do we get from the plant
called *Ananas Comosus*?

0 Pineapple

2 Litchi

3 Paw paw

4 Grenadilla

5 Mango

10 Nectarine

What was the date of the Munich Agreement
signed by Chamberlain, Daladier,
Hitler and Mussolini?

0 30 September 1937

2 3 April 1939

3 30 September 1938

4 30 September 1939

5 4 August 1939

10 3 September 1939

Who was the youngest player ever to have won
the Wimbledon Ladies Tennis Championship?

0 Chris Evert Lloyd

2 Maureen Connolly

3 Pauline Betz

4 Helen Wills

5 Lottie Dod

10 Margaret Smith Court

Who is most likely to know about
Voussoir Stones?

- **0** Landscape gardener
- **2** Jeweller
- **3** Doctor
- **4** Structural engineer
- **5** Sculptor
- **10** Knife-sharpener

In which sport did men compete for
the Jules Rimet Cup?

- **0** Motor racing
- **2** Golf
- **3** Association football
- **4** Polo
- **5** Canoeing
- **10** Fencing

In *A Midsummer Night's Dream*
which of these characters was a joiner?

- **0** Quince
- **2** Snug
- **3** Bottom
- **4** Flute
- **5** Snout
- **10** Starveling

Which wonder of the Ancient World was built
on the instructions of Queen Artemisia?

- **0** Tomb of Mausolus
- **2** Temple of Diana at Ephesus
- **3** Colossus of Rhodes
- **4** Statue of Jupiter Olympus
- **5** Pharos of Alexandria
- **10** Hanging Gardens of Babylon

In which environment
does a jerboa like to live?

- **0** Tundra
- **2** Shallow pool
- **3** Desert
- **4** Ocean
- **5** Marshland
- **10** Rocky mountains

What is the more common name for
the garden flower *Lunaria*?

- **0** Marigold
- **2** Honeysuckle
- **3** Foxglove
- **4** Forget-me-not
- **5** Honesty
- **10** Cornflower

In which country was the
Boxer Rebellion of 1900?
0 China
2 South Africa
3 Serbia
4 Australia
5 Bolivia
10 Alaska

For what feat in 1875 is
Captain Matthew Webb best remembered?
0 Swimming the English Channel
2 Climbing the Matterhorn
3 Walking to Vladivostock
4 Finding an Egyptian tomb
5 Inventing the typewriter
10 Discovering a rare bird

In a modern car, with what do the big-end bearings
come into contact?
0 Crankshaft
2 King-pin
3 Front axle
4 Gudgeon pin
5 Camshaft
10 Rear axle

Who, in Greek mythology, sat at a banquet with
a sword suspended over his head by a single hair?

  0 Damocles
  2 Demosthenes
  3 Procrustes
  4 Democritus
  5 Thucydides
10 Pheidipides

In which country is the unit of currency
one baht equal to 100 stangs?

  0 Brunei
  2 Upper Volta
  3 Tonga
  4 Nigeria
  5 Laos
10 Thailand

Which ballet has the alternative title
'The Girl with Enamel Eyes'?

  0 *Giselle*
  2 *Petrouchka*
  3 *Ondine*
  4 *Coppelia*
  5 *Sylvia*
10 *La Sylphide*

Who called one of his early locomotives
'Catch-me-who-can'?
0 George Stephenson
2 William Symington
3 Richard Trevithick
4 James Watt
5 Robert Stephenson
10 Thomas Savery

What is an ampersand?
0 The sign &
2 Connection to a loudspeaker
3 Hour glass
4 Piece of clear amber
5 Species of tiny crab
10 Small star in printing *

What is the largest cat
of the Americas?
0 Ocelot
2 Cheetah
3 Jaguar
4 Puma
5 Tiger
10 Leopard

What does parmentier imply
in the name of a dish?
- **0** It is sprinkled with Parmesan cheese
- **2** It is served cold
- **3** It incorporates potatoes
- **4** It is sprinkled with parsley
- **5** It is served with a sauce
- **10** It contains mushrooms

Which Christian saint was the mother of
the Emperor Constantine the Great?
- **0** St Cecilia
- **2** St Margaret of Scotland
- **3** St Barbara
- **4** St Catherine
- **5** St Helena
- **10** St Agnes

What is the lowest note on a
normally-tuned violin?
- **0** D (above middle C)
- **2** A (below middle C)
- **3** G (below middle C)
- **4** Middle C
- **5** E (above middle C)
- **10** B (below middle C)

Who landed in Table Bay in 1652
with 90 settlers?

 0 Jan van Riebeeck
 2 Simon van der Stel
 3 James Cook
 4 Vasco da Gama
 5 W. A. van der Stel
10 Bartholomew Diaz

What was the occupation of
Rodolfo Alfonzo Raffaelo Pierre Filibert Gugliemi
di Valentina d'Antonguolla?

 0 Motor racing
 2 Politics
 3 Mountaineering
 4 Portrait painting
 5 Private detective
10 Acting

Where does the monkey puzzle
tree come from?

 0 Chile
 2 Tibet
 3 Cyprus
 4 Lebanon
 5 Easter Island
10 New Zealand

Who wrote 'Gather ye rosebuds while ye may,
Old Time is still a-flying'?
0   Robert Herrick
2   William Shakespeare
3   Robert Burns
4   Robert Browning
5   Percy Thrower
10 Patience Strong

Where would you find the
van Allen belts?
0   In South Africa
2   In the Earth's magnetosphere
3   In an air-conditioner
4   Inside a taxi
5   On a 1930s dress
10 In a lift-shaft

What is a black-eyed Susan?
0   Butterfly
2   Plant disease
3   Snake from South America
4   State flower of Maryland
5   Cocktail
10 Species of koala bear

What is the international registration
letter for cars from Finland?

0 SF

2 FS

3 F

4 FD

5 FL

10 FN

What did Konstantin von Tischendorf
discover in 1844?

0 A distant galaxy

2 A manuscript of the Bible

3 A new filing system

4 A rare mineral

5 An ancient stone carving

10 A cure for housemaid's knee

What country does the word juggernaut
come from originally?

0 India

2 Greece

3 USA

4 Germany

5 Sweden

10 Netherlands

Who is most likely to understand
the Metonic Cycle?

0 Pharmacist
2 Bicycle builder
3 Anatomist
4 Astronomer
5 Drummer
10 Machine knitter

In chemistry, which element has the
lowest atomic number?

0 Oyxgen
2 Iron
3 Carbon
4 Tin
5 Hydrogen
10 Helium

Which of these names was the
nom de plume of Mary Ann Evans?

0 Elizabeth Gaskell
2 E. Nesbit
3 Charlotte Brontë
4 Maria Edgeworth
5 George Eliot
10 George Sand

In which of Shakespeare's plays do the twins
Viola and Sebastian appear?

 0 *Comedy of Errors*
 2 *Twelfth Night*
 3 *As You Like It*
 4 *Measure for Measure*
 5 *The Tempest*
10 *The Winter's Tale*

If you suffer from agoraphobia
what do you dread?

 0 Heights
 2 Wide open spaces
 3 Fire
 4 Knives
 5 Water
10 Confined spaces

What was Bannister's exact time when,
in May 1954, he broke the four-minute mile?

 0 3 min 59.4 sec
 2 3 min 50.0 sec
 3 3 min 59.9 sec
 4 3 min 54.0 sec
 5 3 min 57.9 sec
10 3 min 58.2 sec

Who was the first Independent Labour
Member of Parliament at Westminster in 1892?

0 Sydney Webb
2 Bernard Shaw
3 George Lansbury
4 Keir Hardie
5 Arthur Henderson
10 Ramsay MacDonald

What African bird of prey is known scientifically as
Sagittarius serpentarius?

0 Cassowary
2 Eagle
3 Osprey
4 Hawk
5 Secretary bird
10 Falcon

What is the everyday
word for epistaxis?

0 Forgetfulness
2 Eclipse of the moon
3 Nosebleed
4 Flooding in marshland
5 Bishop's carriage
10 Double exposure of a film

In which engagement was Nelson fighting
when he lost his right arm?

0 Nile
2 Copenhagen
3 Santa Cruz de Tenerife
4 Cadiz
5 Cape St Vincent
10 Calvi in Corsica

Calvin Coolidge became President of the USA
on the death of which President?

0 Wilson
2 McKinley
3 Harding
4 Theodore Roosevelt
5 Hoover
10 Taft

What is the most important product of the bark
of the cinchona tree?

0 Vanilla flavouring
2 Cork for stethoscopes
3 Quinine
4 Ink
5 Stuffing for cricket balls
10 Artist's charcoal

To which of these might the term 'chitting' apply?

0 Marrows
2 Sweet peas
3 Leeks
4 Lettuces
5 Tomatoes
10 Potatoes

What is the name of Europe's largest volcano?

0 Etna
2 Vesuvius
3 Stromboli
4 Hecla
5 Vulcano
10 Thera

Where do Gurkas originally come from?

0 China
2 Nepal
3 Bhutan
4 Assam
5 Thailand
10 Tibet

What would you be most likely to do
with a Sopwith Camel?

- **0** Smoke it
- **2** Stroke it
- **3** Ride on it
- **4** Fly it
- **5** Wear it
- **10** Plant it

Which of the characters in
Pride and Prejudice married Mr Bingley?

- **0** Lydia
- **2** Jane
- **3** Catherine
- **4** Mary
- **5** Elizabeth
- **10** Charlotte

In Greek mythology, what was the name of
Odysseus' wife who unwove by night
what she had woven by day?

- **0** Iris
- **2** Cassandra
- **3** Irene
- **4** Penelope
- **5** Melissa
- **10** Helen

The genus *Tropaeolum* produces a highly-coloured garden flower. What is it called?

0 Polyanthus
2 Geranium
3 Pansy
4 Wallflower
5 Nasturtium
10 Chrysanthemum

Whose book *Profiles in Courage* won the Pulitzer Prize for Biography in 1957?

0 Martin Luther King
2 Alistair Cooke
3 J. F. Kennedy
4 Randolph Churchill
5 Truman Capote
10 Harold Wilson

Who wrote the words of the song which has the refrain 'A policeman's lot is not a happy one'?

0 W. S. Gilbert
2 Harry Lauder
3 George Robey
4 Noël Coward
5 Ivor Novello
10 John Gay

What is the biggest fish in
the world?

- **0** Blue whale
- **2** Narwhal
- **3** Killer whale
- **4** Whale shark
- **5** Beluga
- **10** Greenland whale

Where did the world's first public performance of
a film take place on 28 December 1895?

- **0** Beverley Hills
- **2** Paris
- **3** Rome
- **4** London
- **5** Berlin
- **10** St Petersburg

Who was the founder of
the Jesuits?

- **0** Francis of Sales
- **2** Ignatius Loyola
- **3** Reginald Pole
- **4** Peter Damian
- **5** Philip Neri
- **10** Vincent de Paul

Where were the Olympic Games
of 1936 held?

- **0** Berlin
- **2** London
- **3** Helsinki
- **4** Amsterdam
- **5** Melbourne
- **10** Stockholm

What would you do with a
clarsach?

- **0** Dress it
- **2** Recite it
- **3** Bury it
- **4** Fire it
- **5** Eat it
- **10** Play it

Who was Queen of England for nine days in
1553?

- **0** Henrietta
- **2** Elizabeth
- **3** Matilda
- **4** Anne
- **5** Jane
- **10** Catherine

In which of Charles Dickens's novels
do we find Uriah Heep?

0 *A Christmas Carol*
2 *David Copperfield*
3 *Barnaby Rudge*
4 *Little Dorritt*
5 *Great Expectations*
10 *Oliver Twist*

Who is credited with coining the phrase
'Brave New World'?

0 Lord Beveridge
2 William Shakespeare
3 Marie Stopes
4 Aldous Huxley
5 Lord Longford
10 George Bernard Shaw

Of which country was Bernardo O'Higgins head of
the first national government from 1817–23?

0 Tasmania
2 Greece
3 Chile
4 Alaska
5 Eire
10 Falkland Islands

From which of these places would a coin
bearing an owl be most likely to come?

0 Syracuse
2 Corinth
3 Sparta
4 Macedonia
5 Athens
10 Pergamum

What country is the home
of Shinto?

0 Japan
2 Afghanistan
3 Hungary
4 Indonesia
5 Mali
10 Iraq

In which county is Ronald Blythe's
Akenfield set?

0 Cumberland
2 Dorset
3 Kent
4 Gloucestershire
5 Suffolk
10 Essex

What is a chief interest
of a Sinologist?

0 Crime
2 China
3 Old men
4 Influenza
5 Seals
10 Wine-making

What is a hallux?

0 Nut
2 Bright star
3 Big toe
4 Regimental insignia
5 Firework
10 Lock

Where should you put
a tetra?

0 Inside a piano
2 On an altar
3 Over a bird cage
4 Into a camera
5 Under a mattress
10 In an aquarium

Who was British Prime Minister
at the opening of the First World War?

- **0** Asquith
- **2** Lloyd George
- **3** Bonar Law
- **4** Campbell-Bannerman
- **5** Marquis of Salisbury
- **10** Balfour

If a member of the POEU
comes to your house, what would he do?

- **0** Mend the gas pipes
- **2** Deliver the papers
- **3** Fit a TV aerial
- **4** Fit a tap-washer
- **5** Install a telephone
- **10** Kill the mice

What is an Alaskan
malamute?

- **0** Fur coat
- **2** Hot drink
- **3** Dumb blonde
- **4** Sled dog
- **5** Ice cream cake
- **10** Narrow canoe

Which of these popes
was an Englishman?

0 Pius IV
2 Clement V
3 Adrian IV
4 Leo IV
5 Gregory XV
10 Benedict XII

Whose ancestral home is preserved at
Sulgrave Manor in Northamptonshire?

0 Gough Whitlam
2 Mark Phillips
3 George Washington
4 Charles Darwin
5 W. G. Grace
10 Glenda Jackson

Which river flows 2,300 miles from
the Valdai Hills to the Caspian Sea?

0 Danube
2 Ob
3 Volga
3 Dneiper
5 Oder
10 Neisse

In the centre of which city is
Zadkine's sculpture 'Destroyed City'?
- **0** Dresden
- **2** Stalingrad
- **3** Coventry
- **4** Berlin
- **5** Rotterdam
- **10** Canterbury

Who wrote the novel *Jaws*?
- **0** Peter Townsend
- **2** Peter Lawrence
- **3** Peter Cushing
- **4** Peter Benchley
- **5** Peter Ustinov
- **10** Peter Abelard

Who actually wrote the
Queensberry Rules?
- **0** John Graham Chambers
- **2** Mike McCoole
- **3** Tom Allen
- **4** 8th Marquis of Queensberry
- **5** Ben Hogan
- **10** Oscar Wilde

In which country did
the No Theatre originate?

0 Japan
2 Turkey
3 Norway
4 Iceland
5 Greece
10 No-Man's-Land

What is a basilisk?

0 Egyptian monument
2 Printer's mark
3 Tropical fruit
4 Lizard
5 Nutty biscuit
10 Tree

Which mountain flower is called
Leontopodium alpinum?

0 Edelweiss
2 Gentian
3 Dianthus
4 Sempervivum
5 Rock rose
10 Harebell

What was the purpose of the
Manhattan Project?

 0 To build an arts centre
 2 To protect some Indian tribes
 3 To invent a new hat
 4 To purchase Manhattan Island
 5 To build an atomic bomb
10 To invent a new cocktail

In which country is
Lake Athabasca?

 0 Portugal
 2 Canada
 3 Australia
 4 Cyprus
 5 France
10 Spain

On the reverse of which current British coin
is the thistle royally crowned?

 0 $\frac{1}{2}$p
 2 1p
 3 2p
 4 5p
 5 10p
10 50p

In which country are there administrative divisions called *oblasts*?

0 China
2 Peru
3 Soviet Union
4 Algeria
5 New Zealand
10 Wales

What is the height of the Angel Falls in Venezuela?

0 1,100 ft (336 m)
2 3,212 ft (980 m)
3 980 ft (299 m)
4 612 ft (187 m)
5 511 ft (156 m)
10 1,430 ft (436 m)

Who discovered the Angel Falls in Venezuela?

0 Bartholomew Columbus
2 Christopher Columbus
3 Walter Raleigh
4 Francis Drake
5 Simon Bolivar
10 James Angel

What is 1980 the year of
according to the Chinese?

- **0** Dragon
- **2** Rat
- **3** Monkey
- **4** Snake
- **5** Horse
- **10** Dog

When part of the *Laurus nobilis*
is used for cookery, what is it called?

- **0** Bay leaf
- **2** Dill
- **3** Celery leaves
- **4** Parsley
- **5** Marjoram
- **10** Sweet cecily

In which geological period did
Tyrannosaurus rex live?

- **0** Cambrian
- **2** Jurassic
- **3** Cretaceous
- **4** Carboniferous
- **5** Pleistocene
- **10** Plasticine

What river forms the west boundary of Liechtenstein?

0 Rhône
2 Danube
3 Rhine
4 Neckar
5 Main
10 Severn

In which battle did Davy Crockett die?

0 The Alamo
2 Memphis
3 Stones River
4 Chattanooga
5 Five Forks
10 Seven Pines

What is thiamine?

0 Vitamin A
2 Vitamin B_1
3 Vitamin B_{12}
4 Vitamin C
5 Vitamin E
10 Vitamin M

What is the international registration letter
for cars from Spain?

- **0** SF
- **2** Z
- **3** H
- **4** Y
- **5** E
- **10** S

When people eat skipjack,
what are they actually eating?

- **0** Tuna fish
- **2** Corn flakes
- **3** Tapioca
- **4** Marmalade
- **5** Porridge
- **10** Margarine

Which of these things has the
Vatican City *not* got?

- **0** Hospital
- **2** Prison
- **3** Pharmacy
- **4** Railway station
- **5** Radio station
- **10** Postal service

Who tried to murder his mother by sending her
out to sea in a boat designed to sink?

0 Attila

2 Peter the Great

3 Stalin

4 Dracula

5 Nero

10 Jack the Ripper

Whose autobiography was entitled
Goodness Had Nothing To Do With It?

0 Malcolm Muggeridge

2 W. C. Fields

3 Lord Longford

4 Margot Fonteyn

5 Mae West

10 Michael Parkinson

What is the common name for trees
of the genus *Acer*?

0 Ash

2 Oak

3 Elm

4 Maple

5 Juniper

10 Alder

Name the Earl of Northumbria who was killed
at the battle of Stamford Bridge.

0 Edwig

2 Godwin

3 Harold

4 Tostig

5 Alan Mullery

10 Frank McLintock

What is the astronomical name for the
constellation The Archer?

0 Ursa Major

2 Andromeda

3 Toxophilite

4 Perseus

5 Sagittarius

10 Doris

Who or what is most likely to eat
witchetty grubs?

0 Armadillo

2 Aborigine

3 Three-toed sloth

4 Wild pig

5 Polar bear

10 Yogi bear

Where would platelets
be found?
0 Trees
2 Blood
3 Armour
4 Petrol
5 Circus
10 Beer

Which country has a capital called
Conakry?
0 Sierra Leone
2 The Gambia
3 Guinea
4 Ivory Coast
5 Liberia
10 Eire

Which of these forms part of the head
of all safety matches made in Britain?
0 Carbon
2 Sodium
3 Tin
4 Copper
5 Sulphur
10 Iodine

In which town is there a church tower,
known as the Stump?
- **0** Boston
- **2** Dunkirk
- **3** Ostend
- **4** Boscombe
- **5** Bosham
- **10** Borstal

What is a 'tower of Hanoi'?
- **0** Mathematical puzzle
- **2** Ancient ruin
- **3** Radio station
- **4** Ant hill
- **5** Oil rig
- **10** Instrument of torture

What was General Thomas
Jonathan Jackson's nickname?
- **0** Buster
- **2** Lofty
- **3** Tiger
- **4** Stonewall
- **5** Bomber
- **10** Snowball

What has evolved from
Archaeopteryx?

0 Snails
2 Butterflies
3 Crabs
4 Birds
5 Pigs
10 Batman

Who invented the
hovercraft?

0 Christopher Cockerell
2 Frank Whittle
3 Eric Laithwaite
4 Uffa Fox
5 Werner von Braun
10 Herbert Hover

Who wrote the poem called
'The Rime of the Ancient Mariner'?

0 Robert Southey
2 William Wordsworth
3 Alfred Lord Tennyson
4 Bishop Tenison
5 Samuel Taylor Coleridge
10 Samuel Coleridge-Taylor

What spice is made from the
outside of the nutmeg?

0 Ginger
2 Paprika
3 Cinnamon
4 Mace
5 Cayenne pepper
10 Monosodium glutamate

From which of Verdi's operas does
the 'Anvil Chorus' come?

0 *Nabucco*
2 *Il Trovatore*
3 *Rigoletto*
4 *A Masked Ball*
5 *Falstaff*
10 *La Traviata*

To whom or what did Robert Burns say
'Ye ugly, creepin', blastit wonner'?

0 Mouse
2 Haggis
3 Ant
4 Louse
5 Tam O'Shanter
10 Loch Ness monster

Which king was married to
Caroline of Ansbach?

0 George II
2 George IV
3 William IV
4 Ludwig II
5 Charlemagne
10 King Kong

Which is the capital of
New York State?

0 New York City
2 Albany
3 Utica
4 Syracuse
5 Rochester
10 Buffalo

Which country owned Finland
before it was ceded to Russia in 1809?

0 Prussia
2 Estonia
3 Sweden
4 France
5 Denmark
10 Saxony

Which is the only eagle
nesting in Britain?

0 Bald-headed eagle
2 Martial eagle
3 White-tailed eagle
4 Golden eagle
5 Happy eagle
10 Imperial eagle

What was the occupation of
Paul de Lamerie?

0 Silversmith
2 Soldier
3 Ferryman
4 Cardinal
5 Violin master
10 Chef

What is the minimum percentage
of platinum in a hallmarked object?

0 95%
2 90%
3 75%
4 99%
5 66⅔%
10 50%

What is the 'moonstone' in Wilkie Collins'
novel *The Moonstone*?
 0 Emerald
 2 Moonstone
 3 Opal
 4 White sapphire
 5 Diamond
10 A stilton cheese

What is made by the action of
Streptococcus thermophilus?
 0 Light ale
 2 Bread
 3 Yoghurt
 4 Stout
 5 Rum baba
10 Halva

In which of Jane Austen's novels does
Catherine Morland appear?
 0 *Sense and Sensibility*
 2 *Persuasion*
 3 *Emma*
 4 *Northanger Abbey*
 5 *Pride and Prejudice*
10 *Mansfield Park*

What comes in varieties called
Malling Promise and Norfolk Giant?

0 Loganberries
2 Gooseberries
3 Raspberries
4 Strawberries
5 Blackberries
10 Cranberries

What is fescue?

0 Grass
2 Fine glass
3 Plaited bamboo
4 An old tax
5 Incense
10 Beaten egg-white

In which novel are Fiver and Hazel
the main characters?

0 *Rabbit Run*
2 *The Shrimp and the Anemone*
3 *The Hobbit*
4 *Black Beauty*
5 *Watership Down*
10 *The Scarlet Pimpernel*

Which heir to the throne was killed
by a blow from a cricket ball?

0   Henry Stuart (d.1612)
2   Arthur Tudor (d.1489)
3   Duke of Monmouth (d.1685)
4   Albert Victor (d.1892)
5   Frederick Lewis (d.1751)
10 Leopold (d.1884)

Which country celebrates 14 July
as a national holiday?

0   USA
2   Spain
3   Mexico
4   France
5   Hong Kong
10 Belgium

(The figure in Fahrenheit we all know for normal
body temperature is 98.4°) What is the
normal body temperature in Centigrade?

0   52°
2   26°
3   32°
4   42°
5   37°
10 18°

What name is given to the sweet-scented flower
of the genus *Matthiola*?

0 Stock
2 Peony
3 Lupin
4 Sunflower
5 Foxglove
10 Bluebell

Which film was advertised as the one
in which 'Garbo laughs!'?

0 *Camille*
2 *Grand Hotel*
3 *Anna Karenina*
4 *Ninotchka*
5 *Queen Christina*
10 *Anna Christie*

Who wrote the original story
of *Dracula*?

0 Graham Coker
2 Bram Stoker
3 Mary Shelley
4 Bela Lugosi
5 Bela Bartok
10 Edgar Allen Poe

Where was the opera *Madame Butterfly*
first performed?

0 New York

2 Milan

3 Berlin

4 Paris

5 Venice

10 Tokyo

Which of these chessmen can move
only diagonally?

0 Pawn

2 Castle

3 King

4 Knight

5 Bishop

10 Queen

Who directed the 1930 film
The Blue Angel?

0 Fritz Lang

2 Josef von Sternberg

3 Eric von Stroheim

4 Alfred Hitchcock

5 D. W. Griffiths

10 Walt Disney

Where would you be most likely
to find a Petri dish?

- **0** Laboratory
- **2** Woman's dressing table
- **3** Victoria and Albert Museum
- **4** Chinese restaurant
- **5** Football field
- **10** Television studio

What was the occupation of
Peter Carl Fabergé?

- **0** Piano maker
- **2** Violin maker
- **3** Goldsmith
- **4** Weaver
- **5** Blacksmith
- **10** Shoesmith

Which of these writers does *not*
write science fiction?

- **0** J. D. Salinger
- **2** John Wyndham
- **3** Brian Aldiss
- **4** Isaac Asimov
- **5** Kurt Vonnegut Jr
- **10** Ray Bradbury

What is the chief
constituent of glass?

0 Chromium
2 Silica
3 Calcium
4 Sodium
5 Chlorine
10 Carbon

How many voyages did
Sinbad the Sailor go on?

0 21
2 10
3 13
4 7
5 1001
10 2001

What is the religion
of a muezzin?

0 Judaism
2 Hinduism
3 Islam
4 Jainism
5 Shintoism
10 Christianity

In the stories of Homer, who said to the Cyclops
'No-man is my name'?

0 Ajax
2 Agamemnon
3 Paris
4 Hector
5 Odysseus
10 Telemachus

What popular American composer wrote
'Night and Day'?

0 Cole Porter
2 Lorenz Hart
3 George Gershwin
4 Irving Berlin
5 Stephen Sondheim
10 Leonard Bernstein

Who would know about the
Islands of Langerhans?

0 Physiologist
2 Geologist
3 Ship's captain
4 Petrologist
5 Pearl fisher
10 A mermaid

In the original meaning of the word,
how often should one have a sabbatical year?

0 Every 21 years
2 Every 9 years
3 Every 2 years
4 Every 50 years
5 Every 5 years
10 Every 7 years

In which country is there a large area –
about 250,000 sq miles (647,500 sq km) –
of sand called the Empty Quarter?

0 Egypt
2 Mexico
3 USA
4 Saudi Arabia
5 Iran
10 Australia

Who was the first husband of
Euphemia Chalmers Gray, often called Effie Gray?

0 John Ruskin
2 Edward Burne Jones
3 John Everett Millais
4 Dante Gabriel Rossetti
5 John Keats
10 John Lennon

Who was President of the United States
during the First World War?

0 Theodore Roosevelt
2 Warren G. Harding
3 Woodrow Wilson
4 F. D. Roosevelt
5 William McKinley
10 William Taft

What 1950s pop singer starred
in the film *Jailhouse Rock*?

0 Frankie Avalon
2 Buddy Holly
3 Fats Domino
4 Elvis Presley
5 Chubby Checker
10 James Dean

Whose poem opens with the lines
'Oh! to be in England
Now that April's there'?

0 Browning
2 Keats
3 Byron
4 Shelley
5 T. S. Eliot
10 Shakespeare

From which plant is the
drink tequila made?

- **0** Rye
- **2** Agave cactus
- **3** Corn-on-the-cob
- **4** Sugar cane
- **5** Barley
- **10** Red pepper

In which children's novel does Mary Lennox meet
Colin at Misselthwaite Manor?

- **0** *The Railway Children*
- **2** *Peter Pan*
- **3** *The Borrowers*
- **4** *Mary Poppins*
- **5** *The Secret Garden*
- **10** *Tom Sawyer*

Which conspiracy led directly to the execution of
Mary Queen of Scots?

- **0** Throckmorton
- **2** Babington
- **3** Ridolfi
- **4** Allenby
- **5** Popish
- **10** Gunpowder

In which of Shakespeare's plays do
Touchstone and Audrey appear?

0 *Twelfth Night*
2 *The Winter's Tale*
3 *The Tempest*
4 *A Midsummer Night's Dream*
5 *As You Like It*
10 *All's Well That Ends Well*

Dennis Gabor won the 1971 Nobel Prize for Physics
for the invention and development of holography.
What is it?

0 Statistics chart
2 3-D images
3 Cremation method
4 Instrument for measuring sonic booms
5 Indelible writing
10 Glass cutting

What was the name of
Captain Ahab's ship in *Moby Dick*?

0 *Pequod*
2 *Mary Celeste*
3 *The Bounty*
4 *The Argo*
5 *Cutty Sark*
10 *Mayflower*

Who, in 1897, discovered the
electron?

0 Ernest Rutherford
2 Otto Hahn
3 Max Planck
4 J. J. Thomson
5 Frederick Soddy
10 Albert Einstein

What would you be eating if you had
bouillabaisse?

0 Fruit salad
2 Lentil soup
3 Fish stew
4 Chicken and rice
5 Pasta
10 Lamb stew

Who became known as the
1st Earl of Ypres?

0 Sir Douglas Haig
2 David Lloyd George
3 Sir John French
4 Sir Edward Grey
5 Sir Edward Carson
10 John Buchan

What is ullage?

- **0** Piles of ticker-tape
- **2** Feeling of resentment
- **3** Unused space
- **4** Collection of stones
- **5** Pigeon droppings
- **10** Brake fluid

Where is George Ferris's name best remembered?

- **0** Kitchen
- **2** Hospital
- **3** Fairground
- **4** Greenhouse
- **5** Coal mine
- **10** Printing press

Who had a famous meeting at Guayaquil in 1822?

- **0** Livingstone and Stanley
- **2** Gladstone and Disraeli
- **3** Che Guevara and Fidel Castro
- **4** Bolivar and San Martin
- **5** Laurel and Hardy
- **10** Abbott and Costello

Which famous pair co-starred
in the film *Adam's Rib*?

- **0** Ginger Rogers and Fred Astaire
- **2** Lauren Bacall and Humphrey Bogart
- **3** Jeanette McDonald and Nelson Eddy
- **4** Bette Davis and George Brent
- **5** Katherine Hepburn and Spencer Tracy
- **10** Myrna Loy and William Powell

Who won the competition in 1840 to design the
new Palace of Westminster after the fire of 1834?

- **0** Ninian Comper
- **2** William Butterfield
- **3** Charles Barry
- **4** Alfred Waterhouse
- **5** George Gilbert Scott
- **10** Basil Spence

Of what animals are there breeds known as
Toggenburg and Saanen?

- **0** Goat
- **2** Goose
- **3** Pony
- **4** Duck
- **5** Rabbit
- **10** Sheep

Wnat is the approximate diameter
of the planet Earth?
- **0** 8,000 miles (12,872 km)
- **2** 20,000 miles (32,180 km)
- **3** 2,000 miles (3,218 km)
- **4** 50,000 miles (80,450 km)
- **5** 100,000 miles (160,900 km)
- **10** 1,000 miles (1,609 km)

Who was elected
Lady of the English in 1141?
- **0** Gertrude
- **2** Matilda
- **3** Eleanor
- **4** Hildegard
- **5** Margaret
- **10** Isabel

Which town is at the confluence of the
Tweed and Eddleston Water?
- **0** Peebles
- **2** Tweedsmuir
- **3** Galashiels
- **4** Coldstream
- **5** Melrose
- **10** Kelso

Who would be able to make a
Blintzed Bird Base?

0 Stone mason

2 Venetian blind maker

3 Origami expert

4 Taxidermist

5 Yoga expert

10 Chef

Which saint's day is kept
on 26 December?

0 St Peter

2 St John the Baptist

3 St Stephen

4 St Nicholas

5 St Alban

10 St George

In which of the six counties are Ballymena,
Ballycastle, Ballymoney and Ballyclare?

0 Londonderry

2 Antrim

3 Fermanagh

4 Armagh

5 Tyrone

10 Down

Which city stands on the site of
Tenochtitlan and Tlaltelolco?
- **0** Mexico City
- **2** Bogota
- **3** Lima
- **4** La Paz
- **5** Maracaibo
- **10** New York

Across which piece of water did Kingsford Smith
and Ulm make the first flight in 1928?
- **0** Pacific Ocean
- **2** Atlantic Ocean
- **3** English Channel
- **4** Arctic Ocean
- **5** Irish Sea
- **10** Zuider Zee

Who would have most cause to fear the
Ceratocystis ulmi?
- **0** Zoo keeper
- **2** Milkman
- **3** Probation officer
- **4** Forester
- **5** Lacemaker
- **10** Muffin man

In which county is the
town of Monmouth?
- **0** Gwent
- **2** Clwyd
- **3** Mid Glamorgan
- **4** Dyfed
- **5** Powys
- **10** Gwynedd

What is adobe used for?
- **0** Sailors' laundry
- **2** Making sun-dried bricks
- **3** Starting a car
- **4** Making jam set
- **5** Cleaning silver
- **10** Mending socks

Who was King of England when
Thomas Becket was killed?
- **0** Henry I
- **2** Edward II
- **3** Stephen
- **4** John
- **5** Henry II
- **10** Edward III

What chemical substance usually forms
the 'fur' inside a kettle?

0 Calcium carbonate
2 Sodium carbonate
3 Sodium chloride
4 Lead acetate
5 Calcium oxalate
10 Carbon dioxide

What was the original Alhambra,
built in the Middle Ages?

0 Russian tea-house
2 Finnish sauna
3 Egyptian temple
4 Greek sports stadium
5 German theatre
10 Moorish palace

For what purpose
should you use a wok?

0 Cooking
2 Skating
3 Digging
4 Harvesting
5 Writing
10 Ironing

In heraldry, what colour is meant
by the term gules?
0 Blue
2 Green
3 Red
4 Purple
5 Black
10 White

What is produced as a result
of sericulture?
0 Carved ivory elephants
2 Silk
3 Disease-resistant rice
4 Disease-resistant mice
5 Anti-snake serum
10 Pearls

What is the common name
for rubella?
0 Chicken pox
2 German measles
3 Measles
4 Scarlet fever
5 Mumps
10 Spanish flu

In which of these books does
Lupin Pooter appear?

0 *Catch 22*
2 *The Wizard of Oz*
3 *Zuleika Dobson*
4 *Wind in the Willows*
5 *The Diary of a Nobody*
10 *Confessions of an Opium Eater*

Which gas is most abundant in the
Earth's atmosphere?

0 Carbon dioxide
2 Nitrogen
3 Argon
4 Neon
5 Oxygen
10 Hydrogen

What is the better known name of
Domenikos Theotokopoulos?

0 Tony Curtis
2 El Greco
3 Miki Theodorakis
4 Pope John XXIII
5 Melina Mercouri
10 Rasputin

What do you study if
you are a herpetologist?

- **0** Snakes
- **2** Match-box labels
- **3** Contagious diseases
- **4** Cooking apples
- **5** Bilge water
- **10** Stage costume

Who was the father of
Bonnie Prince Charlie?

- **0** Henry Stuart
- **2** James Francis Edward Stuart
- **3** Lord Darnley
- **4** Charles Edward Stuart
- **5** George II
- **10** Harry Lauder

Which place contains areas once known as
Caelicyth, Chenisitun and Knottynghull?

- **0** Dundee
- **2** London
- **3** Maidstone
- **4** Ross-on-Wye
- **5** Penrith
- **10** Banbury

Who was King of Albania from
1928 to 1939?
0 Michael
2 Constantine
3 Ludwig
4 Sigismund
5 Carol
10 Zog

Who is most likely to use
a Ghiordes knot?
0 Turkish rugmaker
2 Yachtsman
3 Boy scout
4 Candle maker
5 Astronomer
10 Alexander the Great

In Greek mythology, according to a play by
Euripides, Alcestis is willing to die for her husband.
Who is her husband?
0 Alexander
2 Amphitryon
3 Alcinous
4 Admetus
5 Augustus
10 Alvin Stardust

Of which republic of the USSR
is Kiev the capital?

0 Moldavia

2 Ukraine

3 Latvia

4 Georgia

5 Belorussia

10 California

What is a purple hairstreak?

0 Butterfly

2 Tulip

3 Shell

4 Fish

5 Shrimp

10 Beetle

Who was Viceroy of India
from 1925 to 1931?

0 Lord Curzon

2 Lord Lytton

3 Lord Minto

4 Lord Halifax

5 Lord Mountbatten

10 Lawrence of Arabia

Who would use a yealm
in his work?

0 Thatcher
2 Tiler
3 Shoemaker
4 Hedger
5 Ditcher
10 Helmsman

What substance is made
by the Haber process?

0 Common salt
2 Electric power
3 Ammonia
4 Steel
5 Hardboard
10 Butter

What popular red vegetable is in fact the fruit
of the *Lycopersicon esculentum*?

0 Pepper
2 Radish
3 Tomato
4 Aubergine
5 Beetroot
10 Carrot

What creature which comes into our gardens has
the zoological name *Erithacus rubecula*?

- **0** Robin
- **2** Newt
- **3** Fox
- **4** Red squirrel
- **5** Weasel
- **10** Snail

Where is the Great Bed of Ware?

- **0** Fitzwilliam Museum
- **2** Shakespeare's birthplace
- **3** Ashmolean Museum
- **4** British Museum
- **5** Victoria and Albert Museum
- **10** Ware

Where did Churchill, Roosevelt and Stalin meet
on 4 February 1945?.

- **0** Tehran
- **2** Casablanca
- **3** Yalta
- **4** Malta
- **5** Potsdam
- **10** Scarborough

Answers

5 E. R. Burroughs, Hit it (nail), Jocasta **6** .62 mile,
Pacific Ocean, Fourpence **7** Joseph Stalin, Caves, Beetle
8 King David, Judy Garland, Fern collector **9** St Helena,
Colombia, *Saint Joan* **10** Paprika, Stanley Baldwin, Goldcrest
11 Sulphuric acid, Edgar, Ear **12** St Martin, Feet,
Denmark **13** 1644, Petruchio, Isotope of hydrogen **14** Sabrina, Hair, Somalia **15** Antoine Cadillac, Telling the time by water,
5 gm **16** 1750, Orion, Ethiopia **17** Tarragon, Railway
timetables, Nancy Astor **18** 24, Mercury, An officer's thick
overcoat **19** Rice, Choux, Eratosthenes of Alexandria
20 Archbishop of York, Franklin Roosevelt, Christopher Marlowe
21 Frankenstein, Brazil, Heinrich Hoffman **22** Flowering
currant, Quaestor, The Great October Revolution of 1917
23 Vitamin K, Abraham Darby, Dunnet Head **24** Heracles,
238° F, Uranus **25** Wilfred Owen, Citrus fruit, Gandhi
26 Cistercians, Mae West, Juan Manual Fangio **27** Rome,
Harold Lloyd, Samuel Beckett **28** Pittsburgh, Bearded vulture,
Beef **29** Pineapple, 30 September 1938, Lottie Dod
30 Structural engineer, Association football, Snug
31 Tomb of Mausolus, Desert, Honesty **32** China, Swimming the
English Channel, Crankshaft **33** Damocles, Thailand, *Coppelia*
34 Richard Trevithick, The sign &, Jaguar
35 It incorporates potatoes, St Helena, G (below middle C)
36 Jan Van Riebeeck, Acting (Rudolf Valentino), Chile
37 Robert Herrick, In the Earth's magnetosphere, State flower of
Maryland **38** SF, A manuscript of the Bible, India
39 Astronomer, Hydrogen, George Eliot **40** *Twelfth Night*,
Wide open spaces, 3 min 59.4 sec **41** Keir Hardie, Secretary bird,
Nosebleed **42** Santa Cruz de Tenerife, Harding, Quinine
43 Potatoes, Etna, Nepal **44** Fly it (aeroplane), Jane, Penelope
45 Nasturtium, J. F. Kennedy, W. S. Gilbert **46** Whale shark,
Paris, Ignatius Loyola **47** Berlin, Play it (harp), Jane

48 *David Copperfield*, William Shakespeare, Chile   **49** Athens, Japan, Suffolk   **50** China, Big toe, In an aquarium   **51** Asquith, Install a telephone, Sled dog   **52** Adrian IV, George Washington, Volga   **53** Rotterdam, Peter Benchley, John Graham Chambers   **54** Japan, Lizard, Edelweiss   **55** To build an atomic bomb, Canada, 5p   **56** Soviet Union, 3,212 ft (980 m), James Angel   **57** Monkey, Bay leaf, Cretaceous   **58** Rhine, The Alamo, Vitamin B₁   **59** E, Tuna fish, Hospital   **60** Nero, Mae West, Maple   **61** Tostig, Sagittarius, Aborigine   **62** Blood, Guinea, Sulphur   **63** Boston (Lincolnshire), Mathematical puzzle, Stonewall   **64** Birds, Christopher Cockerell, Samuel Taylor Coleridge   **65** Mace, *Il Trovatore*, Louse   **66** George II, Albany, Sweden   **67** Golden eagle, Silversmith, 95%   **68** Diamond, Yoghurt, *Northanger Abbey*   **69** Raspberries, Grass, *Watership Down*   **70** Frederick Lewis, France, 37°   **71** Stock, *Ninotchka*, Bram Stoker   **72** Milan, Bishop, Josef von Sternberg   **73** Laboratory, Goldsmith, J. D. Salinger   **74** Silica, 7, Islam   **75** Odysseus, Cole Porter, Physiologist   **76** Every 7 years, Saudi Arabia, John Ruskin   **77** Woodrow Wilson, Elvis Presley, Browning   **78** Agave cactus, *The Secret Garden*, Babington   **79** *As You Like It*, 3-D images, *Pequod*   **80** J. J. Thomson, Fish stew, Sir John French   **81** Unused space (in a ship, for example), Fairground, Bolivar and San Martin   **82** Katherine Hepburn and Spencer Tracy, Charles Barry, Goat   **83** 8,000 miles (12,872 km), Matilda, Peebles   **84** Origami expert, St Stephen, Antrim   **85** Mexico, Pacific Ocean, Forester (Dutch elm disease)   **86** Gwent, Making sun-dried bricks, Henry II   **87** Calcium carbonate, Moorish palace, Cooking   **88** Red, Silk, German measles   **89** *The Diary of a Nobody*, Nitrogen, El Greco   **90** Snakes, James Francis Edward Stuart, London   **91** Zog, Turkish rugmaker, Admetus   **92** Ukraine, Butterfly, Lord Halifax   **93** Thatcher, Ammonia, Tomato   **94** Robin, Victoria and Albert Museum, Yalta